ETERNAL MAKEOVER

SECRETS TO BEAUTY THAT NEVER FADES

VOLUME 1

Marshelle Barwise

Dream • Pursue • Inspire

ENTERTAINMENT

Heart Entertainment Publishing

Published by Heart Entertainment LLC

Phoenix, Arizona 85041

Heart Entertainment LLC titles are for purchased in bulk for educational, fund-raising, or sales promotional use. For info visit www.marshellebarwise.com.

Unless otherwise noted, Scripture quotations are from the New King James Version. Any italics in the Scripture quotations reflect the author's emphasis.

ISBN 978-0-9982552-1-7
Printed in the United States of America.

#ETERNALMAKEOVERBOOK

You can follow and participate in Eternal Makeover updates by using the hash tag #EternalMakeover Book on social media networks. Please note, this book is the first volume in a mini-series, so keep a look out for new volumes with more great content to help illuminate the timeless beauty you possess.

DEDICATION

I dedicate this book to every person who has ever been made to feel like they had to earn, buy, or borrow something outside of themselves to be deemed beautiful. May these timeless truths bring you the same freedom they bring me every day, and may they take root in your heart so deep that you forever glow like the natural-born beauty you are!

TABLE OF CONTENTS

ACKNOWLEDGEMENTS

With Special Thanks:

This book wouldn't have been possible without the support and encouragement of some very special people.

First, thank you, GOD! You are my motivation, hope, and joy. The only reason I am. Without You, I'd be lost, and every day I wake up thankful I've found true life through a relationship with You.

To my Parents: Thank you for always believing in me and pushing me to share the gifts and creative ideas God has given me. When I'm scared to step out, your steadfast belief in me makes all the difference. Mom, you are so creative and inspire me to do more. Dad, you are so full of wisdom, and I appreciate the opportunities I get to sit down and discuss life with you. You have both shaped me into a better woman. For that, I'm thankful.

To my Husband: Carlos, the way you love draws me closer to the Father. Thank you for holding me accountable and speaking life in me and over me every day. You are truly a vessel God is using to help me navigate through this beautiful life journey. As always, when one of us wins, we both win. So here's to many more years of winning for the glory of God. I love you, *xoxo.*

Sylvia, Beverly, Lisa, Lourdes, and Ms. Cathy: Thank you for believing in me, praying for me, standing with me, and breaking that good word of life with me. You all share the common interest of cornering me to declare that God has a call on my life bigger than my imagination. If every person had a group of individuals like you in their life, the world would be a better place. I love you ladies so much and thank God for connecting our lives to dream big, pursue hard, and inspire together.

To my siblings and loved ones: I'm blessed to call you family and thankful for your continual support. You've all encouraged me on many levels, so I wanted to be sure to acknowledge you in this book. Let's celebrate with a game night. Coleman style!

To my Readers: Thank you for taking the time to share this experience with me. I know my work wasn't in vain even if just one person is touched by what God gave me. I look forward to connecting with you as we journey this road together.

HOW TO READ THIS BOOK

This book was written to unite a community of people who want to express a true definition of beauty. To get the most out of this book, you need to make a prior commitment to engage with the material and take real action towards continuing or starting your journey down the path of eternal beauty. To accomplish this I highly suggest the following:

One: I believe that success is better with the company of others, so read this book with someone else for support and encouragement.

Two: Every page you encounter should be all about you, so please avoid reading this book with a critical mindset only intending to identify errors in me or someone else. If you read anything familiar, ask yourself "*what's something new I can learn from this*." That will open up your mind to new revelation.

Three: This is not a race. Just make sure you see the process all the way through. You can break this down into 13 days, weeks, or months. The goal is just to keep pressing forward.

INTRODUCTION

I've always used writing as a method of therapy and self-reflection. If the piece of work had an actual impact on me, *only then*, would I release it in the hopes that at least one person could gain something good from it.

In this book, I've written down some revelation that I've learned on my journey with Jesus. In the process of completing this work, I was able to witness my very own insecurities depart with every word that flowed from my heart to the page. For that reason, I felt that this book was worth sharing.

Although it wasn't initially written with others in mind, I sincerely pray that God will cause every word to instill His eternal beauty in the hearts of everyone who reads it.

Before you dive into the book, I want to be clear that my intention in writing it was not to imply that I "have it all together," but rather to promote the One who does. I only want to share some good news that I once was deprived of. There are life-changing revelations that can produce an irrevocable beauty that emanates from the inside out, thus making this beauty untouchable and everlasting. I believe I've discovered a few of these truths for myself, and I would like to share them with anyone who is interested.

In a few of the chapters, you will find some "worthy repeat" sections in brackets. For me, a worthy repeat is a share worthy statement and represents a foundational truth that hits the core of the topic being discussed. Therefore, I would highly recommend that you try to lock these in your memory.

You can also find some practical brave beauty challenges on the website to help jump-start your journey with simple calls to action.

Lastly, throughout the book, I will ask you to declare some amazing truths about yourself. I believe that there is power in our words, so I encourage you to say them with boldness in high expectation. Are you ready to start the eternal makeover journey? If so, HERE WE GO!

FOUNDED IN BEAUTY

"We can choose to settle for coal, or surrender to the process it takes to make us a diamond."

PLACE YOUR PICTURE HERE

I encourage you to dedicate this journey to the woman you know you are meant to be.

†

When discussing the concept of beauty, I am challenged to reflect on my journey up to this point.

During my mental journey, I remembered moments of being obsessed with society's definition of beauty, feeling like I had to artificially enhance who I was to fit the standard. Revisiting those feelings of inadequacy along with the external striving for socially acceptable beauty — *you know*, the type of superficial beauty that constantly has to pass the daily visual examination to be considered "good enough" — was not easy. What I know now, but failed to realize at the time, is that the acceptance I was vying for was something that could never fill me, because I wasn't accepting my true self.

The beauty that once came from actually loving and knowing who I was had been replaced by a cruel and critical self-examining attitude. I barely wanted to see my face without makeup, and God forbid that I be seen in public without all of my daily enhancements. It sounds ridiculous, but I know it's a common problem for more people than would admit to it.

If that was, or is, you, this book was not written to be a force of judgment, but more a source of deliverance. These pages are a sacred memoir of confessions beckoning to the hearts of those longing for freedom. Whether you're willing to openly confess your struggle or not, there is a valid form of eternal beauty that can restore what many little girls (or anyone for that matter) lost the first time they were insulted for a physical feature they had no control over like hair texture, skin color, or smile.

These physical qualities meant to graciously distinguish our unique beauty and make us a featured attraction in this God-given journey were misunderstood and identified as a flaw.

It's time to revisit that moment and denounce the lies, to lay hold of the natural beauty that was always meant to be yours from the beginning into eternity.

Otherwise, we will always be living under the oppression of elusive beauty that can never actually be attained. The truth is that there is no single definition of beauty because God only makes custom masterpieces. We were all carefully crafted by the mind of God to be His elaborate demonstration of beauty on Earth.

[**WORTHY REPEAT**: *The truth is that there is no single definition of beauty because God only makes custom masterpieces.*]

"He has made everything beautiful in its time. Also, He has put eternity in their hearts, except that no one can find out the work that God does from beginning to end." Ecclesiastes 3:11

Based upon this verse, our existence alone is beautiful and an eternal mystery. Therefore, our unique attributes shouldn't be a concern, because beauty doesn't define the person — the person defines beauty. We were founded in beauty. It is intertwined in our nature.

When we're unaware of that fact, we search to find our identity from external and artificial things, instead of tapping into the eternal character that God has stored away in our hearts. This truth alone should give everyone a sigh of relief because physical beauty is fleeting and won't last forever for anyone.

So investing our time and energy to maintain something that wasn't meant to last forever is a sure pathway to disappointment.

Now, on the other hand, the character of the heart is the storage room for eternity, and that is what will transcend this life and be the determining factor on how we live out forever. Since God is eternal, anywhere He dwells will be sustained. For that reason, the first and most important step to a timeless beauty that will never fade is giving our hearts to the Sustainer Himself.

[**WORTHY REPEAT**: *Since God is eternal, anywhere He dwells will be sustained.*]

DECLARE: My existence was formed in beauty. Beauty is a part of my nature!

CHAPTER ONE:
THE TRUE MEASURE OF BEAUTY

THE EYE OF THE BEHOLDER.

I'm sure that just like everyone else, you've heard and had maybe even quoted the famous saying, *"Beauty is in the eye of the beholder."*

Although this statement is frequently quoted, I have to wonder if anyone takes the time to reflect upon what it truly means.

The more I think about it, *to me*, it sounds like you can only be beautiful based on the opinion of the person who's looking at you. If that's the case, I'd have to say that beauty isn't reality — it's perception. Why do I say that? Well, throughout a person's life their eyes are being conditioned by education, culture, belief systems, experiences, and environments — so their visual perception is always evolving.

Therefore, I feel we can perceive something to be beautiful, but we cannot declare it as a final decision. Real beauty is irrevocable and is only defined by someone with an immutable nature — and the only one that fits that requirement is God Himself. This could be why the author of Proverbs 31 calls beauty vain.

"Charm is deceitful, and beauty is vain, but a woman who fears the Lord shall be praised." Proverbs 31

With that being said, although our impressive vocabulary and on-point appearance may fool the human eye, there is nothing we can do to fool the eyes of God.

In Samuel chapter one God sent a Prophet to visit the house of Jesse to anoint one of his sons as the next king. Jesse had eight sons, but he only chose to present the seven that he felt possessed the visual "appearance" of royalty. As the first son approached the Prophet, he thought he was looking at the next king; but God quickly confirmed that he was not the chosen son. So one by one, the remaining sons passed before the Prophet until there was no one left. Of course they were all shocked and confused. They thought, "How could this be?" In their eyes, there was only one brother left, and certainly, he wasn't fit to be a king.

What they failed to realize is that the right qualities to be royalty are not found on the exterior. The essential quality required to sustain a position of power is a genuine and transparent heart. So God, knowing their hearts, instructed the Prophet to call for the last son. When he finally arrived everyone was stunned with disbelief, that David, their little ruddy brother, was announced as the next king.

Right now, someone is counting us out because we don't look the part and they may even be trying to pressure us to conform. Of course, we can choose to succumb and start measuring our beauty by societies standard or we can focus on preparing our hearts for the divine appointment of God. This doesn't mean that we have to forsake physical upkeep, so no need to neglect your eyebrows, but what it does mean is that we need to make God's standard of beauty our top priority.

Now if you're anything like me, you might be thinking that fixing your hair, doing some power squats, and putting on some matte lipstick is far easier than addressing the condition of your heart. You're right!

When I started this journey, the condition of my heart and character was a mess, okay, honestly a hot mess, and I'm still walking out my eternal makeover process. Nevertheless, the intangible rewards that have come out of my commitment to this process have been worth it.

Now if you're worried about the depth of your flaws, don't be. The good news is that Jesus Christ already put on the flaws of our human nature to defeat our past, present, and future errors. He offers us an opportunity to put on His eternal glory to experience the life only God can give — which is also where timeless beauty is found. Our part is just choosing to accept His offer and committing to seek His truth to expose the lies about beauty until they're permanently removed from our lives.

DECLARE: I am the apple of God's eye and He defines my beauty. So today, I vow to walk this journey by faith and trust in the Lord's ability to complete the beautiful work He started in me.

CAPTURE YOUR BEAUTIFUL THOUGHTS

1. How do you measure your beauty? (Ex. Social Media, T.V., Family, etcetera.)

_____

_____

_____

2. Have your physical features ever been criticized? If so, how did that affect you?

_____

_____

_____

3. What was your first or most memorable experience with the concept of "beauty"? How did it shape your understanding?

_____

_____

_____

For _the LORD does_ not _see_ as man sees; for man looks at the outward appearance, but the LORD looks at the heart." **1 Samuel 16:7**

REFLECTIVE NOTES

CHAPTER TWO:
THE BEAUTY OF TRANSPARENCY

TOO MUCH CONCEALER.

Remember those scenes in television shows where a teenage girl would be dressed one way in front of her father, but as soon as she left the house for school, she would change her clothes and demeanor?

Well, that's a great picture of what it's like when we adjust our moral stance to fit into the standards of society. This double-minded lifestyle is not sustainable, and it's inconsistent with who we are.

The fact is that our act doesn't fool our heavenly Father. He's just waiting for us to freely expose our true nature and trust Him to lead us into destiny because He only works in truth.

When we feel the need to exist between different alter egos, we subject ourselves to sin through shame, and we choose defeat over victory. For that reason, I encourage you to present the same appearance and posture you carry into the Father's house everywhere you go.

We have no need to live life in disguise or deny the fact that we were in His presence. We have come from Him, and He alone is the source of our eternal beauty. When we are transparent, the irrevocable beauty that we receive from Him as carriers of His image is able to shine through.

"But whoever denies Me before men, him I will also deny before My Father who is in heaven." **Matthew 10:33**

[**WORD OF ENCOURAGEMENT**: When I was a teenager, I loved writing music, and my dream was to become a professional songwriter. In the hopes of being part of a chart topper, I would spend long hours writing and working with a few friends at the studio. One time after my life-changing experience with Jesus, I remember meeting up with a few friends to work on some music. During that session, one of my friends dropped a new beat he had produced, and it was so HOT! Of course, we all got excited and started to brainstorm song concepts. We came up with something catchy, and I wrote a verse. As I got ready to put my two cents in, an unusual statement popped up in my head that I've never thought before: "*Remember whose you are.*" At that moment it felt as if time stopped. I wasn't the same Marshelle anymore, and that thought (which I believe was the Holy Spirit) reminded me. Now, what? Everyone was waiting for me to share my verse, which just a second ago I had been bragging on, but now realized was a denial of the truth. My heart was heavy and conflicted because I was looking back at who I used to be. Prior to my encounter with Jesus it was so easy to write because I could say whatever came to my mind without any accountability. The lives that would fall under the sound of my lyrics didn't matter to me then, but now I felt a higher sense of responsibility.

Nevertheless, my friends were waiting, so I shared the verse. As soon as I said the last word, they went crazy. They loved my lyrics so much they insisted that I record it right away. I was thinking "*Oh no, what did I do? I don't want to put this on a recording to represent me. I don't believe anything I just said. It's all a lie."* Well of course, in the pursuit of looking like the same Marshelle, I recorded the verse, and it spiraled to more explicit lyrics from other contributors.

I left that session feeling like I had failed the Lord and didn't know if I wanted to call myself a believer anymore. But God, in His goodness, just used it to open my eyes to the subtle temptations I might face throughout my life. He helped me realize that I allowed my desire to make music and be a songwriter keep me from proclaiming what I believed. All the while, everyone else was freely standing for what they believed to be true. If you've been there before, I encourage you not to let it bring you down, or pull you back. Just know that the Holy Spirit is present to lead and guide us into truth and that very truth is nothing to be ashamed of because it has the power to set anyone free. For that reason, we can be unashamed to speak, *and more importantly*, live out the truth.]

DECLARE: I am not ashamed to resemble the glory of God because I am a descendant of His greatness. For He is the source of my eternal beauty.

CAPTURE YOUR BEAUTIFUL THOUGHTS

1. What does "being transparent," mean to you?

_____

_____

_____

2. Are there any social settings where you feel the need to conceal your real image?

_____

_____

_____

3. When and where do you feel safe to be 100% transparent? What is it about this setting that makes you feel free to be you?

_____

_____

_____

Therefore, putting away lying, *"Let each one of you speak truth with his neighbor,"* for we are members of one another. **Ephesians 4:25**

REFLECTIVE NOTES

CHAPTER THREE: THE BEAUTY OF YOUR TESTIMONY

A TOUCH OF PERFECTION.

As I wrote this work, it occurred to me that most women, including myself, have a lot in common with the woman in the Bible with the issue of blood. If you haven't read that story, I encourage you to do so. It can be found in *Mark 5:25-34*.

The story talks about a woman who had a heavy flow of blood for 12 years. Since blood carries life, *in essence*, it's safe to sum it up by saying she had issues overflowing in her life that she could not stop. There was no relief. She sought professional counsel, medical care, and practically spent all her money to end up with no resolution.

Talk about disappointment. All those systems are supposed to fix the mess, right? Wrong. There are some matters in life that only Heaven has an answer to, and none of those methods could help her because the cause of her external condition was an internal issue. And because of her condition, this woman was eventually isolated in society and unable to freely walk out her purpose. I remind you, it was 12 years of this affliction.

[**WORTHY REPEAT:** *There are some matters in life that only Heaven has an answer to.*]

As you can imagine, she experienced loneliness, singleness, and probably feelings of worthlessness. It's likely that everyone, including her, believed that she'd have to continue to live like this and eventually die like this. But one day, after many years of affliction she chose to disregard how everyone else had labeled her and decided to press her way to peace. The Prince of Peace to be precise. That was the day she came into contact with Jesus, *and in an instant*, her 12 years of issues were dried up. The power of Jesus healed her completely. She was forever changed.

Just like that woman, my relationship with Jesus has healed many problems in my life, including my need for external validation, which He has replaced with freedom to pursue the seemingly impossible.

I know that many women have experienced being overwhelmed by issues in this life, whether they were physical, mental, spiritual, emotional, or relational. Luckily, the answer hasn't changed. The Prince of Peace, Jesus, is still accessible and able to produce healing in an instant. The only thing required is our belief and willingness to reach out to Him for help. If you're feeling overwhelmed by the issues of life, rest assured that you're not alone. Jesus suffered every hurt humanly possible and every day countless people have to endure the unpleasant hardships of life.

I can personally tell you that the majority of what I've written in this book came out of periods in my life where I had an issue that required me to press past every external force to connect with Jesus. If this resonates with you, right now is an opportune moment to lay aside your label, recognize your limitations, and relentlessly reach for Him. It's as easy as setting your thoughts on Him and genuinely speaking out your need for His help and healing. By faith, draw everything you can from Him to the point that He responds "who touched me." The fact is that He wants to be touched by you and He is waiting to meet your needs and more — that way you can tell the world another account of your beautiful testimony.

[**WORD OF ENCOURAGEMENT**: In November 2015, I started to get ill. I had every possible symptom you could imagine from shortness of breath, tremors, chills, stomach pain, body aches, brittle bones, fatigue, loss of hair, rapid weight loss, no appetite, random bruising, neck pain, severe head pressure, headaches, and the list could go on. In the onset of the symptoms, I did everything I thought could swiftly make this go away. In other words, I visited a medical center and received testing that showed my blood was healthy. That was a relief, but that report didn't change my symptoms, so they put me on antibiotics. I followed the protocol for four days until I started getting, what felt like, brain crushing headaches. I also began to get heart racing so bad that one-day I stayed up for 36 hours in fear that I'd die if I went to sleep. I was exhausted, and I had enough, so I threw away the remaining pills. After that, my husband and I agreed that we needed to take this before God and use healthy food to aid my body - so he made fresh vegetable and fruit juices for me daily. We also stepped up our regular encounters with God and started focusing on prayer, worship, declaring words of healing over my body, and I even received intercession from ever prayer warrior I knew. Nothing changed. How could this be? So, in desperation, I instantly turned into a Google monster. You know, when you start looking up all the possible outcomes according to Internet experts. The results led to confusion and more fear. The fear led to anxiety and depression. At that moment I understood why some people would prefer not to be alive anymore. The mental torment kept my mind fixated on death and disease, and I eventually lost sight of my hope and future (Jer. 29:11). It was a scary place to be. Despite all the people I had prayed for with confidence that God would come through, for some reason in this instance, I couldn't do it for myself. I felt like the authority we all have in Christ Jesus through the blood and the power of our testimony dissipated from me. I lacked spiritual endurance, and instead of continually working to build it up in the Word, I became desperate and started looking in any and all directions for an answer. I spent tons of money going to the Doctors for various test and counsel, which only made me more frustrated and disappointed in the sometimes carelessness of society. As a result, I started to become very critical of people in help services for not having the ability to do what I thought they existed for - saving me. I eventually received a report that I had an abnormal disorder that could turn into something fatal. It was confirmed that there was nothing any person could do to change my situation (Sigh). My weary journey to find healing through practical knowledge (which does have some benefits) brought me back full circle. I started to reflect on the promises of God and His design of creation. My restored focus on God was the beginning of renewed peace and hope for a future. No, my situation still isn't perfect, but that doesn't mean that my focus needs to drift from the perfect One. Psalms 103: 2-4 reads, "*Bless the Lord, O my soul, and forget not all His benefits: Who forgives all your iniquities, who heals all your diseases, who redeems your life from destruction, who crowns you with loving kindness and tender mercies.*" God will always remain faithful to His Word. He cannot lie, so during the storm and when it has passed, God will still be there as our Redeemer ready to crown us with more loving kindness and tender mercies. Our job is to believe and never give up!]

He who dwells in the secret place of the Most High Shall abide under the shadow of the Almighty. I will say of the LORD, "He is my refuge and my fortress; My God, in Him I will trust." **Psalms 91: 1-2**

DECLARE: I have overcome by the blood of the Lamb and by the word of my testimony. No matter the test, I vow never to give up on God and believe that He will never give up on me.

CAPTURE YOUR BEAUTIFUL THOUGHTS

1. Reflect on a difficult moment in your life that may have caused a season of isolation, loneliness, or pain.

2. How has that painful life experience help build your character?

3. After experiencing that trial, what beautiful expression of encouragement can you now share with someone who is currently going through a similarly hard time?

_____

_____

_____

_____

_____

_____

And they overcame him by the blood of the Lamb, and by the word of their testimony; and they loved not their lives unto the death. **Revelations 12:11**

<u>REFLECTIVE NOTES</u>

CHAPTER FOUR:
THE BEAUTY OF BEING GENUINE

DON'T PUBLICIZE, PERSONALIZE.

We all know that successfully presenting a fake image in front of people is a piece of cake! That's because no one can see your heart; they only see the actions that you choose to present. So just step out in your most stylish outfit, perfectly laid hair, and "hide it all" smile. If you don't show it, they won't know it. *But who are you when no one is watching?*

What if everyone had to have their private life evaluated in comparison to their public life? How many surprising discoveries would be made? That's a personal question that most people don't explore because the reality may be scary to face. It was this dual lifestyle that I once lived, and now daily defy, that is a sure pathway toward destruction.

While God remains the same yesterday, today, and forever, people are always changing. The way we think and what we like can be one thing today and entirely different tomorrow. God is as solid as a rock and provides a sturdy foundation. On the other hand, people who live by their desires can be likened to an unstable bridge that is suspended thousands of feet in the air and being swayed by the wind. On many occasions, I trusted the opinions of people over the Word of God. I have walked that bridge and have fallen into the deep abyss. All the signs were present, but my prior awareness still didn't stop me from moving forward, nor did it prepare me for the feelings of profound devastation that I experienced.

I can tell you that many of my greatest disappointments in life so far have been the result of my trying to live up to or down to what other people thought of me. I have now learned that living by human opinion is unstable and possibly the most dangerous path to travel down.

[**WORTHY REPEAT**: *Living by human opinion is unstable and possibly the most dangerous path to travel down.*]

The most consistent way to find identity and purpose is through personalizing our walk before the Lord. Only the One who sees all, knows all, and is in control of all is fit to examine our lifestyles. This is not to say that you should never consider someone else, so please don't use this as an excuse to be arrogant. But what it does mean is to be careful not to fall into the tendency of behaving a certain way based upon what others may think. We should ever be mindful to measure our thoughts about life up to the Word of God. Taking on the mentality that if it does not align, then it's no longer mine and immediately dismiss the lie from our life.

You find that some people are trustworthy, but we should never trust anyone over God, that even includes ourselves. The word is clear in Romans 3:4 *"Let God be true but every man a liar."* So, no matter who's holding the opposing view to what

God has said, God is true, and the opposing side is always the liar.

[**WORTHY REPEAT**: *You find that some people are trustworthy, but we should never trust anyone over God, that even includes ourselves.*]

GENUINE LEADERSHIP

Everyone is in a position of leadership in some form or fashion, especially in this day and age with social media.

The leadership roles could be wife, mother, doctor, teacher, preacher, artist, follower of Christ, business owner — and the list could go on. Regardless, the moment you reveal your title, people will have preconceived notions about who you are and how you should conduct yourself.

This is why it's easy for leaders to fall into the trap of acting out what is considered their *role* or *title.*

Be it a great title or not, what people call you could start conditioning your mind to live up or down to what they label you as. If you're not careful, your title could even enslave you.

Therefore, continually being mindful that our life is from God and for God (Col. 1:16) is what will empower us to resist the pressure to live out the expectations of people.

[**WORTHY REPEAT:** *Continually being mindful that our life is from God and for God is what will empower us to resist the pressure to live out the expectations of people*.]

This understanding requires a humble disposition. So if any leader, including myself, assumes that this understanding has no relevance, it could be a sign that we are more likely to fall into the trap of a "public persona" lifestyle. We cannot allow ourselves to be deceived. A real leader is a constant learner and should always stay humble before people, and most importantly, before the Lord.

So in the process of leading, we should be careful not to deem ourselves exempt from the truth that we encounter and share. It is not okay to tell our children to "*do as I say and not as I do.*" That is not the heart of God or the example of Jesus.

The truth is a powerful force of existence, and no one is exempt from it. So simply speaking the truth does not excuse us from having to live the truth. We should stay open to godly correction at any level in life and always be looking for ways to gain new understanding.

"Understanding will keep you." **Proverbs 2:11**.

Everyone in existence has a call to celebrate the truth; even if we weren't the one used to say it, and recognize that hearing something we have heard as an opportunity to expand our faith (Reference Rom. 10:17). With the mass of ongoing lies in the world today, the truth should never be treated like old news, *but rather* it is to be reverenced, every time it is heard.

[**WORTHY REPEAT:** *If something is true it should always be reverenced no matter how many times it has been heard.*]

DON'T CHASE PRAISE.

I know all too well what it feels like to want to be validated. Hearing positive feedback produces a good feeling, especially if it comes from someone whom you admire. And of course, no one intends to feel like his or her life is insignificant. Nevertheless, no matter who it is that is validating us, our concern of their opinion should be of less value than God's viewpoint regarding our life.

This would be a good moment to ask ourselves if the characteristics we display, to maintain the titles we have, are genuine. Are we publicizing to brag on our accomplishments, or is this a genuine walk of faith before God?

Life is too short to be living out the role that someone else is trying to have you play in his or her scripted life story.

No matter how well it's planned out, it will never stack up to what the Alpha and Omega has carefully crafted for our existence. The story that God wrote for us is phenomenal and if we choose to trust in Him, not a single detail of our life will be lost, because we are His original workmanship, being recited into the universe for such a time as this (*Ephesians 2:10 reference*) .

If you know that you've been living out of alignment with God's will for your life, it's time to ask Him how you can get back on track for the extraordinary story He has composed for you.

Living a life constantly aware that God is always watching, and choosing to live an honorable life before His sight, is the key to a journey of victory. An accountability partner to help you stay committed to a life of integrity is valuable as well; however, that should never replace maintaining a genuine reverence for the presence of God on a daily basis (*Matthew 10:26 reference*).

DECLARE: I am His workmanship, created in Christ Jesus for good works, which God prepared beforehand that I should walk in them. **Ephesians 2:10**

CAPTURE YOUR BEAUTIFUL THOUGHTS

1. What titles have you commonly been labeled with?

2. How have those titles impacted your behavior?

3. Who do you have in your life right now that can hold you accountable to remaining true to who God called you to be?

_____

_____

_____

_____

_____

_____

_____

_____

_____

_____

For His eyes are on the ways of man, and He sees all his steps. **Job 34:21**

REFLECTIVE NOTES

CHAPTER FIVE:
THE BEAUTY OF DEVOTION

*"My son, give attention to my words; Incline your **ear** to my sayings. Do not let them depart from your **eyes**; Keep them in the midst of your **heart**; For they are life to those who find them, and health to all their flesh. Keep your heart with all diligence, for out of it spring the issues of life. Put away from you a deceitful **mouth**, and put perverse lips far from you. Let your eyes look straight ahead, and your eyelids look right before you. Ponder the path of your **feet**, and let all your ways be established. Do not turn to the right or the left; remove your foot from evil."* **Proverbs 4:20-27**

BE DEVOTIONAL, NOT EMOTIONAL.

Our emotions and thoughts are always being bombarded by daily outside influences. These outside influences try to forge themselves in our lives through our senses. If they gain access to our senses, they try to create confusion to distort the original image we were created in. From the beginning of existence, this assault against our emotions has been happening and will continue to happen throughout our lifetime.

So why is there such an attack against our emotions? This is something I have always wondered about.

From birth, all of our senses are activated so that we can experience the pleasures that come along with being alive. Our senses are a gift from God. He created us with the ability to experience life in 3D High Definition. However, failure to protect our senses (i.e., *see, taste, touch, smell, hear*) from unhealthy and harmful exposure can open us up to the bait of short-term pleasure with long-term pain attached. This is the experience of a fish that is lured by a quick meal dressed to appear as instant gratification with no cost. Unfortunately, after one bite the fish discovers the meal was good, but that the hook attached will cost its life. The sad reality is that humans have been using the same bait to catch fish for centuries, and *yet*, fish do not have the intellectual ability to figure it out. Now although we are not fish by nature, we can become as foolish as baited fish if we choose not to learn from past failures.

[**WORTHY REPEAT:** *Failure to protect our senses (i.e., see, taste, touch, smell, hear) from unhealthy and harmful exposure can open us up to the bait of short-term pleasure with long-term pain attached.*]

The act of esteeming our devotion to God above our feelings and sensations, or better yet, *sin-sations* that try to carry us away from His will, is a critical component to staying clear of the bait. That is why the first instruction that Adam was given by God in the garden directly spoke to protecting his senses. We find this out from Eve when she tells the serpent, *"God has said, "You shall not eat from it, nor shall you touch it, lest you die"* referring to the tree in the middle of the garden (*Genesis 3:3*) .

Things haven't changed since the beginning. We are still instructed to guard our senses to avoid the crafty deceit of the enemy. To this day, he is still using the same lie to recreate his plan of defeat from generation to generation. His plan is to restrict us with limitations through unhealthy affections (2 Corinthians 6:12). But by entering into a relationship with Jesus Christ, we are empowered to overcome the lies of the enemy. Our strength and safety come from remaining rooted in God through abiding in faith, hope, and love.

[**WORTHY REPEAT:** *Our strength and safety come from remaining rooted in God through abiding in faith, hope, and love.]*

These three are a shield of defense against disturbing emotions such as fear, doubt, hate, confusion, and despair, which try to overcome us in life and distort our beauty.

The Word is also an anchor that gives us stability to trust God, even when our environment is trying to convince us that He is a liar who intends to keep us from something better.

His Words are for our protection. The documented story of creation gives proof to humanity that God should always be trusted. To stand in opposition and test God on His Word is to re-invite deception and death into our lives.

DECLARE: I will walk in the beauty of devotion and take authority over my emotions by guarding my senses from the bait of unhealthy *sin-sations*.

CAPTURE YOUR BEAUTIFUL THOUGHTS

1. What time and days can you set aside to intentionally spend devoted time with the Lord?

_____

_____

2. What methods do you currently use to evaluate your emotional state and how it's impacting your faith walk?

_____

_____

3. Are there any reoccurring traps you continue to find yourself in? If so, what has been the device used to lure you down the path and what can you do differently to prevent it from happening again?

_____

_____

If anyone among you thinks he is religious, and does not bridle his tongue but deceives his own heart, this one's religion is useless. **James 1:26**

<u>REFLECTIVE NOTES</u>

CHAPTER SIX:
THE BEAUTY OF DISCIPLINE

DISCIPLINE IS THE KEY TO PROGRESS.

Now let's talk about our part in this walk of faith: self-control. At the beginning of creation, out of His giving nature, God gave humankind dominion over the earth (Genesis 1:26). Since God is committed to His Word, He sustains the foundation of the world, but we are responsible for its maintenance (Colossians 1:16-17). That's why God will keep us, but He will not control us.

[**WORTHY REPEAT**: *God will keep us, but He will not control us.*]

The ability to choose is another gift from God (Deuteronomy 30:19-20). Now, of course, it is apparent to an all-knowing God that He is the best choice, but we have to make the decision to invite

Him into our lives personally. When we invite Him into our lives, we gain access to His everlasting life and goodness again. So, the question is, why wouldn't everyone want to experience this goodness? Great question. Let's glance back to the very beginning again.

In the book of Genesis, Adam and Eve, the representative of humanity, started out in perfect relationship with God. In this relationship, as the Ultimate Creator, God gave them some clear instructions on how to live life with peace and complete provision.

It may be hard to imagine, but they had absolutely no needs because they were all met through their relationship with God. Even more, because they were in the Will of God, the enemy could not touch them.

One day, the enemy cunningly took on the form of something that appeared familiar, a serpent, and slithered into the Garden of Eden. Just like he still does today, the enemy then used the weapon of lies and deception in hopes of creating division between Adam, Even, and God. Tragically, through Adam and Eve's failure to remain disciplined to the instructions of God, sin was introduced in the earth. And as a result, a seed of deception was engrafted in the heart of humanity and the only thing that could destroy it was an even stronger incorruptible seed.

"Having been born again, not of corruptible seed but incorruptible, through the Word of God which lives and abides forever." **1 Peter 1:23**

The account of Adam and Eve is still being played out in the present day. The only thing that may have changed is the image the enemy takes on. Instead of being a serpent he may use our feelings or the most popular of them all: cultural norms. Just like in the garden, he creeps into the church, your job, the media, or even your household and plants a mental seed of doubt to spark division. A common example of this is when we think we are better than other people for futile reasons like economic status, race, education, appearance, and etcetera. The subtle feeling of superiority is just one example of the lies that the enemy has devoted his existence to spreading, so that he can keep humanity in bondage and disrupt our ability to relate to one another. The only thing we can do to counteract it is to remain disciplined to the Word, will, and plan of God. Otherwise, we will get stuck living life void of the benefits God intended for us to experience. Therefore, even if we are saved by grace, we still have to maintain the faith and walk out the process of God's will on earth. This requires us to trust in Him despite what we see or feel — now, into eternity.

DISCIPLINE OVER DEFEAT

The greatest weapon that the enemy uses against us is our very own senses. Remember, the enemy is not a creator — he's just crafty. That is why he needs our help to accomplish his destructive plans. It's also important we realize that the enemy doesn't control our feelings, and neither does God, we do! Therefore, the next time we pop off on someone, we can't blame it on the enemy. We made the choice not to practice our peace. Our ability to choose is the reason why God's forgiveness still doesn't exempt us from having to go through the consequences, because otherwise, we would never learn from our mistakes. The consequences are a reminder that we need to discipline ourselves and choose to practice God's principles in every situation.

[**WORTHY REPEAT**: *The enemy is not a creator — he's just crafty.*]

Now, keep in mind that the enemy just recycles his same methods, with different devices, to create stumbling blocks in our walk of faith. He implements the same plan he used in the beginning. First, he comes in disguise, because he never wants us to know who he is — in fact; his goal is to make us believe he's non-existent.

To overcome this tactic, we need to invest time in learning about God and what He says about us. As we learn, it is important to exercise our faith by following God's Word to see it work on our behalf.

I remember when the Lord told me to sell my beautiful home in a down market. I was not thrilled to act in obedience knowing that I would take a financial loss and I currently had no place else to stay. Nonetheless, during a time of prayer I heard the Lord say "*When you do what I say, you will see what I can do*." I didn't want to take another risk on testing God's perfect plan for my life because I'd recently been there and done that and knew the results weren't good. So I acted in faith and started to pack even before I got a call back from the realtor to sell. Long story short, it was later through selling the house that led me to get a better job and eventually to meeting my husband. And to think, I was actually questioning God's plan for my life in that moment.

My experiences have taught me that when we put time into becoming familiar with God, it becomes less likely that someone (or our own misleading thoughts) will be able to deceive us into believing that something good is evil or that something evil is good. Every day, we need to discipline ourselves to seek God's Word for answers and trust Him above all, so that not even our social surroundings or the most charismatic speaker can convince us to believe another false gospel (Galatians 1:6-12).

Another tactic the enemy tries to use is deceptive pleasures or pride to convince us that our want is a need.

His plot is to get us to expose our senses to the perversions of life so that we'll evoke unhealthy feelings and emotions inside ourselves (i.e., pain, confusion, bitterness, premarital lust, etc.). Whether we have accepted Christ already or not, unhealthy sin-sations are always a tactic used by the enemy to put a wall of separation between God and us. This is seen in Isaiah 59:2, which reads "But your iniquities have separated you from your God; and your sins have hidden His face from you so that He will not hear." Willingly engaging in sin is communicating that we want to be estranged from God.

To resist and overcome the enemy's pride and pleasure tactic, we must discipline ourselves to daily conform to the Word and not the world by filling our lives with activities that accomplish God's will for our lives (Romans 12:2, 1 John 2:15-17, Philippians 4.8). And even when temptation appears to have us cornered, remember that God always provides a way of escape from the temptation of sin (1 Corinthians 10:13). We just have to choose to take it.

Last but not least, let's learn from the discipline that Jesus displayed during His life on earth, which led to the remissions of our sins. Through His life and sacrifice, we are able to confess our faults from a sincere heart to regain access to our eternal beauty. That is because He is faithful and just to forgive us and cleanse us from all unrighteousness through His never ending love (1 John 1:9).

In closing of this chapter, it is still up to us to operate in self-control to resist the enemy's tactics. If we do our part to remain disciplined in submitting to God in sincere devotion, we will be empowered to resist the enemy, and it is guaranteed that he will flee.

If we choose not to resist, we will have to endure the consequence and may never experience the abundant life that Christ has made available to us right now. It's ours, so let's go get it!

[**HIGHLIGHT VERSE**: Therefore submit to God. Resist the devil and he will flee from you. **James 4:7**]

[**HIGHLIGHT VERSE**: God frustrates the devices of the crafty so that their hands cannot carry out their plans. **Job 5:12**].

DECLARE: I will not allow myself to be deceived by the sin-sations of this world. I will guard my heart, mind, soul, and emotions against perversion and seek out the truth through God's Word.

CAPTURE YOUR BEAUTIFUL THOUGHTS

1. What areas of your life lack discipline?

2. What is something that God has instructed you to do that you have yet to follow through on? Why have you procrastinated?

3. Write down anything that resonated with you from this chapter. Then spend some time reflecting on why it may have stood out to you.

_____

_____

_____

_____

_____

_____

_____

_____

But I discipline my body and bring it into subjection, lest, when I have preached to others, I myself should become disqualified. **1 Corinthians 9:27**

REFLECTIVE NOTES

CHAPTER SEVEN:
THE BEAUTY OF FAITHFULNESS

A FAITHFUL LIFESTYLE.

After we accept the proposal of salvation through Jesus, the relationship with the Lord is likened to the union of marriage. When He looks at us, He sees His covenant and declares "You are altogether beautiful, my love; there is no flaw in you" (*Songs of Solomon 4:7*). He continually states who we are meant to be until we believe it ourselves. He is our head covering and provider. Our part is to keep the lines of communication open, contribute to maintaining the beauty He has lavished upon us, and invest our life in the relationship, just as He has.

With all my admitted imperfections I have to ask myself, am I upholding my part of this relationship? Am I faithful? In all honesty, I have fallen short in my contributions to the relationship. Even still, God has given us His name; therefore, He remains faithful because He cannot deny Himself (*2 Timothy 2:13*).

[**WORTHY REPEAT**: *God's love for us is consistent and unchanging, but it is our love for Him that waivers and causes issues in the relationship.*]

Truthfully, the topic of emotional control to remain faithful is a serious matter, especially if we think regarding marriage. A lot of divorces today are the result of someone choosing to act out of character based on how their *"feelings"* change. Feelings are going to change; that's what they do. We have to discipline ourselves to remain faithfully devoted, despite our emotional inconsistency. Feelings and emotions that are not operated in self-control can enslave us, and even cause us to make a mockery of our relationships and our true identity.

[**WORTHY REPEAT:** *Feelings and emotions that are not operated in self-control can enslave us and even cause us to make a mockery of our relationships as well as our true identity.*]

It may sound like something that can be easily detected before it gets to that point, but the process of emotional bondage is usually very subtle. For example, it may start with something you glanced at or that you overheard. Although it seemed very innocent, suddenly this visual or audible object starts to become a picture in your mind. Next, you then form a small thought regarding the object. If you choose not to dismiss this thought from your life immediately, this object can become a fixating idea. The idea then gets attached to an emotion, causing you to feel a certain way every time you just think about it. Before you know it, the power of imagination takes effect, and you start to fantasize about an interaction with this object of fixation. Finally, one day you are somehow faced with the opportunity to experience the physical reality of what you have imagined. Coincidence? I think not. But since it has become so real and alluring in your mind, you figure you might as well try it. No one will ever know, right? Wrong. What you were going to try just this one time privately, has now integrated itself into your lifestyle or has maybe even replaced your true identity altogether to make a public mockery of YOU.

That is the frequently traveled road of self deception starting with a seed planted in our senses from the enemy. We then choose to water it with our imagination and words, until it becomes a full-grown action.

Does that sound familiar to you? It sure does sound familiar to me. I have been down this road a few times. It's an easy pathway to follow, but turning back from it is a struggle. This is what I would describe as *"Emotional Chaos*," where *sin-sation* latches itself within us. The danger is that it becomes tough, almost impossible, to denounce something corrupt once it has thoroughly disguised itself as the core nature of who you are. In other words, as your identity. And at this point, you feel the need to convince everyone else around you that something corrupt is natural and "beautiful," because you don't know how to separate yourself from this feeling and lifestyle. Friends, don't be deceived; sin is after us, and its assignment is to persuade us to make a covenant with a lie to leave stains of shame on our beauty (Genesis 4:7).

[**WORTHY REPEAT:** *The danger is that it becomes tough, almost impossible, to denounce something corrupt once it has thoroughly disguised itself as the core nature of who you are.*]

Even more, *sin-sation* attracts the company of others who live similar lifestyles. This new found company then justifies their lifestyle, by verbally approving the deception you have now begun to believe about yourself. As we continue to taste-test temptation, the internal sensors we continually chose to ignore that were triggered to warn us that we are headed down a dangerous path are now deactivated by our choosing to permanently deviate from the safety zone God set (*Reference Romans 1:17-32*).

If this sounds familiar to where you're at or where you're headed, I encourage you to stop what you're doing and spend some time with God in prayer. Remember, *if we confess our sins, He is faithful and just to forgive us our sins and to cleanse us from all unrighteousness (1 Timothy 1:9).* The sin is only yours if you choose not to denounce its right to your life, but you can opt to give it to God and be free from it.

If necessary, I would even recommend that you reach out to someone that you can trust.

It goes without saying, but emotions that we fail to control can run a profound and dark work of destruction. This is a direct result of the fall of humanity. I have lacked self-control in my life on many occasions. As a result, I became a puppet to my sin-sations to the point that I acted out of character to please and appease my unhealthy urges (in other words, lustful desires).

Somehow, I fell for the age-old lie that God did not think out every part of my life, so I needed to make it happen. Of course, I found out the hard way, by having premarital sex, drinking to the point of drunkenness, conjuring up lies about someone else to defame their character and feed my pride, and the list can go on. By the way, if you just gasped based upon what I said, just be happy you aren't God because He knows all my dirt (*Reference Hebrews 4:13*). That's why it's beyond pointless to try to pretend before Him. No matter who you are, no one can excel to the point that they do not need to rely on God every single day of their life.

[**WORTHY REPEAT:** *No matter who you are, no one can excel to the point that they do not need to rely on God every single day of their life.*]

I repeat, we need Him in every moment and every single day of our lives. Even with consecutive seasons of victory in our lives, the level of need for God remains the same as the day we first received Him — if not more. I will cover this more in the section of "Living and Leading with Humility."

As a young girl, my mom made it a point to bring me up in the church. She was an excellent example of what it meant to live a life of humility. I learned a lot through those years, but I did not gain much understanding, so the change wasn't evident. It was not until the age of 19 that I truly discovered the life and love of Jesus. I experienced an amazing and life-changing encounter at a youth camp retreat called Elevate. From that moment, I understood the significance of His existence, death, and miraculous resurrection. His life was the eternal symbol of God's love for humanity and our complete redemption from the fall. In Him, the love of God was demonstrated to give us access to a new life if we **choose** to receive it (*2 Corinthians 5:17*)

That revelation was my saving grace. The new life gained through a relationship with Jesus was exactly what I needed. I needed an internal transformation to unearth and heal the deeper things that eyes could not see. The hidden things instilled in me from childhood that had the potential to completely corrupt my hope for the future and replace my God-given beauty with ashes. But praise the Lord, through the help of Jesus, I faced the unhealthy feelings I suppressed and denounced their right to my life and future. This process was not easy, and it has yet to end. As long as we are alive, we are gently refined by the love of God. He is faithful. He loves without sleep and never slumbers (*Reference Psalms 121:3-4*), and although He uncovers our mess, it is never to expose us.

[**WORTHY REPEAT:** *And although He uncovers our mess, it is never to expose us.*]

He reveals the mess to relieve us from the tiresome cycles of defeat and hiding so that He can replace it with freedom if we let Him.

One of the most amazing things about a relationship with Jesus is that nothing in life could separate us from His love *(Romans 8:39)*. When it comes to what He loves, He will not let go, and He will not give up. He is resilient. Even the things we have done that may make us disgusted with ourselves; they do not intimidate Jesus. That is because Jesus knows the beauty that is hidden beneath the mess.

God doesn't lie, and in the beginning, He declared, *"It was very good"* when He made us. As we continually confess our need for Him and denounce our need for anything contrary to Him, this inner work evolves into an outward expression demonstrating exactly what God saw when He said "It is good" *(Genesis. 1:31)*. Through a lifestyle of faith, the weight and pressure of life can be lifted. If we stay faithful in our commitment to God instead of getting carried away by our emotions *(Hebrews 12:2)*, we can then realize the complete rest that comes from trusting in the Lord as the Author and Finisher of our faith (*Hebrews 12:2*).

As believers, we also must be mindful of our need to assert authority over our emotions routinely. Otherwise, we get in the habit of measuring the presence of God in our life by the way we feel. This is how emotional experiences can become a distraction or even an idol. God is not controlled by our feelings. In fact, any relationship in our lives controlled by feelings has a very slim chance of survival.

Earlier in my relationship with the Lord, this misunderstanding deterred my faith at times because to engage with God I had to *"feel"* His presence. Many of you may know the feeling I'm talking about… that goose bumps, warm-hearted, peaceful feeling. If I had those feelings, I believed God was with me — although I often experienced that same feeling when I looked at a delicious meal.

I'm only trying to say that feelings alone are untrustworthy. Our relationship with God is meant to include all of our heart, soul, strength, and mind *(Luke 10:27)*. If we want to overcome the emotional struggle and live a faithful life, we must bring our thoughts and emotions under submission to the Word _daily_.

I cannot say that I've reached a mastery level in this area of my life yet, but I do strive to grow every day. One thing I know is that thoughts and emotions are powerful, so it takes a conscious effort to avoid becoming a puppet to them. Therefore, I will share a few practical tools I try to use in my life.

For starters, memorizing key Bible verses that address my struggle and flood my life with positivity has helped. If you would like to try this method but you don't own a Bible or even know where to look in the book, no worries. You can easily do an online search. For example, if you struggle with depression, you can do a search for Bible verses about joy. Then, once you find those, write a few verses down and commit to meditating on them every day. You can also listen to positive audio like motivational speakers and inspirational music. Lastly, and most important, remove anything that feeds the hurt, pain, stress, or trauma you are feeling out of your life. Some things you dismiss from your life will be temporary and others permanent. This includes people, places, and things. The goal is only to focus on whatever things are true, noble, lovely, pure, and of good report (Reference Philippians 4:8). Note: If it's a person inside your household, it may be wise to pray and seek godly counsel from someone who loves you. If you involve a person, make sure they know how to seek the true heart of God and not just speak from opinion.

Ultimately, bringing our thoughts and emotions under submission will allow us to simultaneously develop our heart, soul, strength, and mind to access the powerful and prosperous life we were created to live.

If our heart condemns us, God is greater than our heart and knows all things *(1 John 3:20)* . Therefore, our commitment should not be based on emotions, but instead, it should be a daily choice to remain firm in our faithfulness to the Lord in all things about life. The result will be that He will surely see us through the hardships of this journey to ensure that we experience and enjoy the pleasure of His promises.

Friends, it is time to start taking account of our emotions and asking ourselves why are they there, and if they're unhealthy, how did they get there?

The plans and promises of God are worth it and are waiting for us to claim them by just following through on His will for our lives.

DECLARE: No matter how I feel, I will remain faithfully devoted to the Lord. I will submit my will and watch Him bring me out victorious.

CAPTURE YOUR BEAUTIFUL THOUGHTS

1. Is there anything in your life that tries to challenge your faithfulness to God? If so, write it out. Example: Career, relationships, dreams, and etcetera.

2. Our thoughts play a significant role in our actions and overall relationship with the Lord. If you examine your thoughts, what excuses typically pop in your mind when you are pursuing faithfulness to God over everything else?

3. The change starts in your heart and mind. Diffuse the excuses that bombard your mind by writing out "why" your relationship with God is worthy of your faithfulness.

This process should be elaborate, so write your answers out on a separate sheet of paper.

If we are faithless, He remains faithful; He cannot deny Himself. **2 Timothy 2:13**

REFLECTIVE NOTES

CHAPTER EIGHT:
THE BEAUTY OF THE TRUTH

"The truth is everlasting, and it doesn't change just because we do." (Reference Psalms 117:2)

SEEK TO LIVE AND SPEAK THE TRUTH.

First, let me just say one of my pet peeves is when someone says, *"I'm the realest person you've ever meet. I don't have to lie."* It's like "yeah right," everyone in life has told at least one lie. I would be lying if I said that I never told a lie. That's some truth for you!

My cover up for lying used to be that if Rahab could do it and save her whole family, then a little lie for a good reason isn't a bad thing. Yes, I tried it.

Thankfully, I've come to learn that a life built on lies is an unstable ground to walk on. The entire world fell in the beginning, all because of a lie. And that same lie from the beginning, that *we don't need God* is still causing many to fall into destruction.

[**WORTHY REPEAT**: *I've come to learn that a life built on lies is an unstable ground to walk on.*]

When we get in the habit of telling little lies here and there to make ourselves look and feel better (because that is the most common reason people lie) we set ourselves up for a fall, and only God knows how many other people it'll affect. Even more, Jesus is the Word of truth, so when we promote a lie, it is the same as denying Jesus because the Word of truth is the essence of who He is. And lastly, since the truth is eternally undefeated, trying to uphold the lies in our life only sets us up for a truth TKO — aka, the total knockout.

[**WORTHY REPEAT:** *Since the truth is eternally undefeated, trying to uphold the lies in our life only sets us up for a truth TKO — aka, the total knockout.*]

The greatest evidence that one stands for the truth is that they live by the truth that they proclaim. There is no greater example than a living example that is why what was once a mystery became clear after Jesus appeared as the expressed revelation of the Word (*John 1:14*).

Still today, the world we live in is looking for living examples — especially if we're a proclaimed believer. For that reason, it's necessary that our lives take on a pure form of transparency in the presence of the multitudes. After all, we are NOT the standard, Christ is, and we are simply commissioned to follow after Him.

[**WORTHY REPEAT:** *We are NOT the standard, Christ is, we are simply commissioned to follow after Him.*]

During the process of faithfully following Jesus, He performs the work of making our lives an example before our generation. So with that, we can all take a deep breath, remove our knockoff super savior cape and pick up our little crosses with humility.

Now, should we fail to live out the truth, it's our responsibility to confess that the truth is still accurate – as opposed to discrediting the truth to justify our wrongs and cover our reputation. Remember, "*Let God be true but every man a liar (Romans 3:4)."*

[**WORTHY REPEAT:** *If we fail to live out the truth, it's our responsibility to confess that the truth is still accurate - as opposed to discrediting the truth to justify our wrongs and cover our reputation."*]

The truth is also beneficial, because when we have sin to hide, the hidden holds us captive to the fear of being exposed. Fear then becomes a restricting force that prohibits growth in specifics areas, if not in all areas of our life.

I cannot tell you how many times I have been held back by the lies and fears I allowed to remain active in my life. Even now, the feelings of fear still try to hold me back at times. My fear of people's opinion was the reason this book was delayed. But fortunately, God put a stop to that, and now here you are holding the results of my faith in His promises.

The only two forces on earth that are stronger than fear are truth and love. The truth provides freedom, and love provides safety. Lies have no more authority when you speak the truth, and love covers you to provide safety and security. This is the reason why confession is so powerful (*we will discuss this in detail later*)! Exposure of the darkness releases us from its hold and gives light permission to illuminate our lives. Not to mention, living a life built on the truth establishes an atmosphere of peace around us.

[**WORTHY REPEAT:** *Living a life built on the truth establishes an atmosphere of peace around us.*]

So if you, just as I have on many occasions (so definitely no judgment), have lies causing darkness in your life that are placing a force of restriction against you reaching your destiny and being able to receive the will of God — there is no better time than now to humble yourself and confess the truth. Yes, it will be scary, and maybe even embarrassing.

Those are the natural emotions that fear produces to prevent the truth from being spoken. Just remember, *there is no condemnation to those who are in Christ Jesus (Romans 8:1).*

You may even feel like you will be rejected, but *If we confess our sins, He is faithful and just to forgive us our sins and to cleanse us from all unrighteousness (1 John 1:9).* And once you receive that God is for you, that is all you need (Reference Romans 8:31).

The truth releases freedom and forgiveness, which means that God's acceptance is waiting on the other side. So don't delay, speak the truth against every lie right now. Once you have laid the truth out before the Lord or even before a sincere person you can trust – make a commitment to live life differently for His glory. Ask God to help you walk in authority, to overcome the wayward *sin-sations* of life that once easily enslaved your mind, body, and emotions. You already know where that will get you, nowhere! But instead, avidly start seeking God's will to avoid being a serial offender.

If you are someone who has once confessed the sin before but have a tendency to hold onto the lie (or sin) as a part of your lifestyle, you are still allowing access for the same occurrences to replay in your life. With God, there is no such thing as partial freedom, and it's much harder to forgive something that someone will not let go of. If you want to be free to experience freedom, you must completely let it go. Take a moment to ask God to help you let it go completely. God is faithful, and He'll meet you where you are.

[**WORD OF ENCOURAGEMENT:** Whether it has been months or even years that you have struggled with this crippling fear, just know that God is not intimidated by the longevity of your darkness or sinful lifestyle. Yes, you may have learned how to adapt in that environment and feel like you're life is unrecoverable, but you have to remember that God is eternal. With just your humble confession before Him, God can defeat the years of your sin in an instant. The span of time you place before Him is and will always be minuscule. Time will never overwhelm God because it isn't for God, it's for us.

It's our constant reminder of how precious life is so that we never get too comfortable and decide to stop moving forward towards purpose and the freedom that awaits us. Break free from fear today, by unleashing the power of "truth".]

DECLARE: Lord, I will no longer live in fear and allow shame to define who I am in this world. I declare that I am your beautiful creation and I will live by your truth to display what you say about me. Now I ask that you fill me with love for Your truth, so I can grow into the likeness of Christ my Redeemer and the Savior of the world.

CAPTURE YOUR BEAUTIFUL THOUGHTS

1. What lies (if any) are trying to hold you captive?

_____

_____

_____

2. How did these lies gain access in your life?

_____

_____

_____

3. What truths (if any) have you been denying to cover your own reputation?

_____

_____

_____

For the LORD is good; His mercy is everlasting, and His truth endures to all generations. **Psalms 100:5**

<u>REFLECTIVE NOTES</u>

CHAPTER NINE:
THE BEAUTY OF HUMILITY

LIVING IN HUMILITY WHILE LEADING IN VICTORY.

The world may see our long list of accolades and be very impressed by our ability to lead. However, we should never allow these types of recognitions to cause amnesia about who the real source of our victory is — God.

The starting point to the pathway of real success is first humbling ourselves and admitting our personal defeat and need for God. The title that we carry and the achievements that we make have no influence on the way that God sees us. That's because He can see past all of our filters and public personas.

[**WORTHY REPEAT:** *The title that we carry and the achievements that we make have no influence on the way that God sees us*.]

We have all encountered people who seemed to be very genuine, but later were exposed to have hidden motives. If only we had the ability to see their hearts, we would have known to protect ourselves from them, right? Well God does not only see our hearts, but He knows the full span of our lives. Out of our heart flows the real nature of who we are and what we believe.

That is why God does not bother to examine our actions or our intentions. His concern is when He looks at our heart, what does He see?

Does He see a congruency between what we say and what we do? Does He see His Word or does He only see our prideful plans? David says, "*Your word I have hidden in my heart, that I might not sin against You*" **Psalms 119:11.**

Sin and pride is a heart issue. So God wants to know, what is the condition of our hearts?

The Bible is full of recorded incidences in history where great kings with endless victories, a mass of wealth, and great possessions fell to nothing in an instant. To us, the defeat they experienced appears to have happened suddenly. But to an all-knowing God, it is likely that the process of failure started within their hearts long before it occurred in a physical sense. The same sudden defeat still happens to people in positions of power and influence nowadays.

Therefore, considering that we are unable to see our hearts, it is necessary to place ourselves humbly before the Lord to be readily available for examination, no matter how highly-esteemed we become in this life.

God's examination of our heart is for our good, but it's also for His glory, and His desire is for us to keep a humble heart.

Humility is simply a constant reminder that it's not me — it's Him. It knows how to receive compliments for success graciously, but yet freely relinquish that praise and give it to God, because it belongs to Him. He just allows us to share in the experience because He loves us — and that's what love does, it gives. So when we experience the blessings of God and refuse to give it back due to a prideful heart, we inevitably set ourselves up for a fall. So in this world built on self-boasting, I encourage you to choose to be humble before the Lord, so you don't have to be humbled by the Lord.

DECLARE: I set my heart to understand and to humble myself before God, so He will hear my words and send angels to war on my behalf. *(Daniel 10:12)*

CAPTURE YOUR BEAUTIFUL THOUGHTS

1. Where in your life have you allowed pride to creep in?

2. In what situations do you find it more challenging to walk in humility?

3. Write down anything that resonated with you from this chapter. Then spend some time reflecting on why it may have stood out to you.

_____

_____

_____

_____

_____

_____

_____

But he who is greatest among you shall be your servant. And whoever exalts himself will be humbled, and he who humbles himself will be exalted. **Matthew 23:11-12**

REFLECTIVE NOTES

CHAPTER TEN: THE BEAUTY OF COMPLETION IN CHRIST

LOSE THE COMPETITION MENTALITY.

The quickest way to become impaired on your journey to greatness is to start comparing yourself to someone else. Now, this isn't to be confused with being inspired by someone, because competition is an entirely different thing.

[**WORTHY REPEAT**: *The quickest way to become impaired on your journey to greatness is to start comparing yourself to someone else.*]

Someone inspirational makes you want to push harder to become the best original version of yourself. Their journey of accomplishment encourages you to pursue your purpose boldly, and that's natural. Competition is to covet someone's position and desire to become "*better than*" them in that regard. There's a thin line between inspiration and competition. The transition occurs when we start to covet the lifestyle that others are living.

Let me put this into perspective. Just think back to any moment where you've seen people receiving praise for something they've done, and the thought popped up in your mind that you could do it too. Their accomplishments may have helped open your eyes to what you are capable of; if so, that's great! But if you're not careful, that thought can quickly progress into "*Mmhm, that isn't nothing*, I *can do better than that*."

Suddenly all the reasons why you're a more deserving person starts to flood your mind. Have you been there before? I admit, I have. Even during my faith walk, I remember one particular moment when the Lord abruptly stopped me in my thought process and made me aware of this toxic thinking. It was a humbling and a very critical time in my walk.

Some of you might be wondering, "What's wrong with saying that you can do something better if it's true?" The problem is that, in a sense, it makes the other person your rival and we aren't to be divided because we are on the same team.

And if Jesus didn't go into his calling of ministry by telling John the Baptist to move out of the way because He was more gifted; then we most certainly shouldn't be doing that to anyone either.

God has a plan for every failure and success. Even more, it could be that our lack of discipline, endless excuses, and need to focus on what everyone else is doing has made us unfit for the success God wrote in our journey. Ouch!

God has created us to be uniquely different for the purpose of fulfilling our personal call in the Kingdom. When our eyes are dangerously positioned on someone else, we are not able to tune into what God is trying to tell us, to go to where He wants to take us.

Jesus is our prime example of having confidence and completeness in His identity. Everywhere Jesus went people were trying to alter who He was and get Him to take another path to purpose. The church leaders and educators were constantly trying to compete with Him because they were jealous of His influence and effortless authority. Other people were always trying to compare Him to prophets and leaders of the past. Obviously, Jesus had plenty of moments where He could have gotten caught up in the competition, but He chose to stay firm in God's plan for His life.

He understood that focusing on someone else's path would distract him from seeing what was ahead on His own beautiful and exciting journey with God.

The ongoing lie of the enemy is that we can't all be blessed because there is not enough to go around. In the mind of many women, the myth circulates that we can't all be beautiful because only one can be the finest. Not true!

In the physical world, the resources are insufficient for the needs of everyone, and that is why people desperately fight over material possessions through war, deceit, and manipulation. In the Kingdom, there is an abundance of supplies to meet EVERY need, because poverty is not a Kingdom trait. In Luke 12:22-31, Jesus tells us not to worry, because the Father knows our needs and will take care of us. This still stands.

If you happen to be down to what seems like your last penny and feel like the world is falling apart, I know this is easier said and read than done. I've been in seasons of faith where I had no money, no job, no home, and belief in God was my only hope. No exaggeration. It was in those moments that all my hopes in material possessions were exposed, and a new foundation of my life was established.

Friend, we don't have to covet what anyone else has. When we ask and believe, God is trustworthy and will show up every time to prove that He is ALL we need. If He says "...Man shall not live by bread alone; but by every word that proceeds from the mouth of God" (Deuteronomy 8:3), then He's going to show up to prove that His Word is a sufficient resource if that's what you're trusting in. He will not be made a liar.

[PRAYER FOR YOU (Read out loud in agreement with me): *God, I'm praying for my friend reading this book who is going through the wilderness of life right now. I lift up my faith on their behalf because I know that you promised never to leave us or forsake us and we trust you. In faith, we lay the needs before you (**Speak all the <u>needs</u> you have out loud**). We believe that you are more than capable of providing these needs and thank you in advance for coming to the rescue. We also ask that you reveal your will at this moment and allow this to produce a testimony of power and a story of victory that brings Your name glory. Enable my friend to rest in your completion and experience your peace that surpasses all understanding within their heart and mind. We ask all this in Jesus' name, Amen!]*

With high expectation, list all the needs you just spoke out loud and revisit this to check off the prayers as God answers them.

Request _____

Date Req._____Date Answered_____

Request_____

Date Req._____Date Answered_____

Request_____

Date Req._____Date Answered_____

Remember, God is faithful and able, so make sure you are prepared to listen for His direction and walk in obedience. If you have praise reports you'd like to share, feel free to send them to us at www.marshellebarwise.com. Your personal win is also a Kingdom win!

God is the Creator of everything, and just by one word God can transform a life. In fact, God has already put a collection of life-changing words before us, and they will prove to be true if we try it. In Christ Jesus, we become members of the Kingdom and family of God, and we are no longer limited to the resources of this world.

[**WORTHY REPEAT**: *God has already put a collection of life-changing words before us, and they will prove to be true if we try it*.]

To operate in the abundance of Kingdom resources and to start experiencing expansion on earth, we have to change our perspective from competing to complete. A vivid example of the competition mentality is the historical record of Cain and Abel. We know that Cain killed his brother Abel out of jealousy. Instead of evaluating his brother's life and allowing him to be a source of inspiration, Cain killed Abel to eradicate the competition. This did not solve anything; it just drove him deeper into darkness.

[**WORTHY REPEAT**: *To operate in the abundance of Kingdom resources and to start experiencing expansion on earth, we have to change our perspective from competing to complete.*]

This scenario is still happening today all over the world, even in the Kingdom of God. The same applies when we badmouth someone, downplay their achievements, purposely refrain from supporting someone to prevent their success, and so on.

Family and friends, earthly blessings are great, but the eternal blessings we inherit are of a far more excellent value and need to be exposed to those who have yet to receive the gift of life through Christ.

Contrary to popular belief, God's will is not to make us rich or establish our name, ministry, family legacy, net worth, networks, events, church congregation, or make this book a best seller — everything God purposes is to advance the kingdom as a whole. One life touched from our assignment is significant to God. Yes, we all know that the presence of God always blesses every area of our life, but misunderstanding the root reason why keeps us from being effective.

An actual blessing is something that reveals a truth about God and gives us understanding on how that truth applies to our life. Everything God does is for the Kingdom to be revealed on earth, and that is why we need to guard ourselves against competing over useless things.

[**WORTHY REPEAT**: *An actual blessing is something that reveals a truth about God and gives us* *understanding on how that truth applies to our life.*]

We have no reason to compete. When we are in Christ Jesus, we are complete. Receiving the acceptance and completion that comes through Christ is the first step to realigning our life to the correct path and breaking free from the limitations of this global system. So together, let's put this unhealthy, limiting, and prideful mindset of competition behind us, and press toward the Kingdom purpose. #TheEternalMakeover

[**SCRIPTURE:** *"...Take heed and beware of covetousness, for one's life does not consist in the abundance of the things he possesses." Luke 12:15*]

DECLARE: In Christ, I am complete, and I have no reason to compete. There is a plan, purpose, and assignment for my life. I am already blessed because God made me and I believe I have access to unlimited resources from Heaven. So, Lord, thank you in advance for all the answered prayers and fulfilled promises that lay ahead of me. I know that those who wait on You will not be put to shame.

CAPTURE YOUR BEAUTIFUL THOUGHTS

1. In what situations do you commonly find yourself starting to compete with others? Why?

2. What are you trusting God to complete in your life? Write it out. Nothing is too hard for God, so remember to dream big and ask from a pure heart.

_____

_____

_____

_____

Then the Lord answered me and said: "Write the vision and make it plain on tablets, that he may run who reads it. For the vision is yet for an appointed time; but at the end it will speak, and it will not lie. Though it tarries, wait for it; because it will surely come, it will not tarry. **Habakkuk 2:2-3**

REFLECTIVE NOTES

CHAPTER ELEVEN:
THE BEAUTY OF ORDER

RELIGION VS. RELATIONSHIP.

The entire journey of life from beginning to end revolves around connections and the people we relate to. Every day we experience the tangible and intangible sensations of life through the relationships we choose to engage in. Relationship through intimacy is also the original design for human reproduction. It is for that reason I confidently state that God's greatest gift to us in life is relationships and what God always intended for us to experience.

[**WORTHY REPEAT**: *God's greatest gift to us in life is relationships*.]

In the book of Genesis, in the beginning, after speaking everything into existence, we see God decides to create something on earth that could resemble and relate to Him. As God holds a conversation with the Host of Heavens, He announces His plan to fashion humankind in a likeness similar to His own.

Why would God do that?

I believe it's because the ability to relate is the key component for a relationship; therefore God's decision to give us attributes that resembled His likeness was evidence of His intention to engage in a relationship with humanity. So if a relationship was the intention, that raises the question, how did the idea of religion come about in connection with God? We will discuss that, but first, I want to start with the order of relationships and then explore the topic of boundaries.

In life, there are four primary forms of relationships you can engage in. All four are significant and should be valued, but the order of priority is what matters the most because the one you choose to establish your foundation will play a significant role in shaping your worldview on everything around you, including yourself.

The four primary relationships in life are:

You + God

You + Yourself

You + Others

You + Creation

Various orders people use:

TOP			
CREATION	OTHERS	MYSELF	GOD
OTHERS	CREATION	GOD	MYSELF
MYSELF	GOD	OTHERS	CREATION
GOD	MYSELF	CREATION	OTHERS
BOTTOM			

Our ability to love and be loved is contingent upon the relationship we choose as our foundation because that relationship is our sustaining factor.

As you can see, there are various ways that they can be stacked. I have personally interchanged the order of these relationships on multiple occasions in my life. I admit that I have put myself first and related to everyone in perspective to how it benefited me. I thought I was superior to everything, but this was draining and unhealthy for my relational life. I have also put others first, but this slowly drifted me into a people-pleasing state and left me feeling just as drained if not more than when I put myself first - because it's impossible to please everyone. So through transitions in my life, I have found one specific order to provide the most stability, and that is by making God my priority and foundation relationship.

It made sense to me that God, being eternal with an unchanging nature, could be an endless source of stability and guide to setting proper boundaries. God as my foundation has allowed me to maintain a better and more harmonious connection in each of the other relationships. Much of that has to do with the fact that He created everything in existence, so my stated honor for Him automatically holds me accountable to honor everything that carries His image and fingerprint.

Okay, so now that I've been open about me, how do you stack them?

What have you set as your priority relationship and defining foundation of life? What is your foundational source and driving motivation for existence? If it's not God, I encourage you to put Him first and watch everything in your life gradually come into order.

DECLARE: God I put you first and trust that you are aligning my life with your perfect will.

CAPTURE YOUR BEAUTIFUL THOUGHTS

At this very moment, what order do you stack your primary life relationships in? Write it out and explore how each relationships position is impacting your life right now. For example, what does your primary relationship take from you and what does it give to you?

_____

_____

_____

_____

_____

_____

_____

_____

_____

_____

_____

But seek first the kingdom of God and His righteousness, and all these things shall be added to you. **Matthew 6:33**

REFLECTIVE NOTES

CHAPTER TWELVE:
THE BEAUTY OF BOUNDARIES

Boundaries - (a) *Something (such as a river, a fence, or an imaginary line) that shows where an area ends and another area begins. (b) A point or limit that indicates where two things become different. (Ref.* Merriam-Webster Dictionary)

SET YOUR BORDERS.

When something is of significant value, it must be protected, which is where boundaries come into play.

For personal use, society loves boundaries. We set boundaries on our money, material belongings, and even on our minds.

Relationally, we verbalize our boundaries by saying what we will not put up with.

On a larger scale, the system of government is no different. In every country laws are established to set boundaries and a variety of consequences are attached to those boundaries in case they are violated. Many laws in society may even be partial to benefit a particular group of people over another, and yet, we comply. So if you thought this was a new concept, think again. The idea of boundaries is widely accepted in the world and considered necessary to provide "protection" to humanity.

Now, if a complex YET limited creation can see the importance of boundaries, why is it a surprise that God, who created everything, has set boundaries as well? In fact, God set boundaries before humanity was even created and they, too, were established for our protection.

GOD'S SOVEREIGN BOUNDARIES.

[**THOUGHT:** It's important NOT to confuse the boundaries of God with the rules that people have established in the name of God. There is a difference.]

Could you imagine if everyone had to live his or her entire life in literal darkness, unable to see the world surrounding us? No colors. No smiles. No visual picture of the purity witnessed in a newborn baby's eyes. No light, just darkness. Thankfully God was considering our experience and journey before He even placed us in the earth. As the gracious God that He is, He wanted us to experience the fullness and goodness of the land that He planned to place us in, so He gave us light and divided darkness to distinguish the difference between the two as referenced in Genesis 1:2-4. See the passage below.

"The earth was without form, and void; and darkness was on the face of the deep. And the Spirit of God was hovering over the face of the waters.
(3) Then God said, "Let there be light"; and there was light. (4) And God saw the light, that it was good; and God divided the light from the darkness."
Genesis 1:2-4

In a similar manner, He also put boundaries on water. Now, some may see water as harmless. Just something that we drink to refresh ourselves or maybe the beach comes to mind. Harmless, right? Well, according to the U.S. Geological survey, about 71 percent of the Earth's surface is water- covered, and the oceans hold about 96.5 percent of all the Earth's water. Wow! Those are some high percentages and they don't even consider water vapors from the sky or the portion that living beings carry.

Plainly put, water is a powerful force that is capable of causing a lot of damage any time it rises well beyond the normal perimeters we are used to. So what is keeping water from completely overpowering the earth and flooding the entire world like it once did in the days of Noah?

Well, I'm sure there is a very compelling scientific explanation, with terminology to match, on how that is so... and I would love to hear it; I would even respect the findings. But I would still say those factors wouldn't explain why? So I'll make a suggestion on why the elements science has discovered, continually hold water in place. According to Genesis 1:9, God set a boundary on where water could flow and made a promise with the rainbow as His symbol of a covenant that even if the waters did overflow onto land, it would never flood the entire earth again (*Genesis 9:13-16*). That promise remains in good standing.

"Then God said, "Let the waters under the heavens be gathered together into one place, and let the dry land appear"; and it was so." **Genesis 1:9**

"The rainbow shall be in the cloud, and I will look on it to remember the everlasting covenant between God and every living creature of all flesh that is on the earth." ***Genesis 9:16***

All of these examples in creation clearly demonstrate the necessity of boundaries, so we must also evaluate our lives to see where we may need to put some boundaries up. After all, our lives are valuable enough that God sent Jesus to save us. His life was a valuable investment for a Kingdom family – which is why it is only right that we act like the royal heirs and heiresses that we are.

PRACTICAL EMOTIONAL BOUNDARIES

The best place to start enforcing boundaries is with our ears, eyes, and mouth. That's because a majority of the turmoil that enters our lives comes from something we heard, seen, or said. Therefore, we should be careful not to entertain anything that is in opposition to the truth we stand for.

[**WORTHY REPEAT**: *We should be careful not to entertain anything that is in opposition to the truth we stand for*.]

For example, I use to love watching television and especially reality shows. As I looked at these shows filled with stupid fights and backstabbing, I'd convince myself that I was just trying to stay current on the cultural changes going on around me. But we all know the truth is that I found these crazy shows entertaining, and so, in the name of entertainment I willing put down my boundaries and granting these shows open access to my eyes and ears. Surprisingly, before I knew it, some of the signature phrases they used were coming out of my mouth. Then some of the styles they wore, were finding its way into my wardrobe.

I was so emotionally open that I started to find myself getting upset with people that I only knew via television. The craziest part is that the process was so subtle that I didn't even recognize that it was happening.

Well, one night I sat down to watch one of my favorite television shows when a thought popped into my head "How can you say that you disagree with adultery if you continue to look at a show that celebrates a man having an affair?"

Now I knew this thought didn't originate from me because I loved this show. So when I tell you, I sat completely still in utter silence for a good five minutes, debating if I'd pretend like I didn't have the thought I am not exaggerating. This is an example of godly conviction. Once again, God was gently reminding me about the importance of protecting my senses to preserve my character and guard my heart. Yes, I had countless excuses pop in my head to justify why I should keep watching the show, but I chose obedience. From that point forward, although I was occasionally tempted, I never watched that "very addicting" show again.

So, you may be asking yourself what this has to do with beauty and boundaries. Everything.

1 Corinthians 15:33 says "*Do not be deceived: "Evil company corrupts good habits.*"

This verse is talking about more than just people. "Company" can also refer to the negative thoughts or lies we entertain, the music we listen to, the shows we watch, the people we adore from a distance and even follow on social media. Anything we occupy our time with that does not align with Philippians 4:8 can become "bad company." Put it this way; our life is like a garden, and it is only going to harvest the type of seeds planted. If the people, thoughts, and things we grant access into our lives plant foolishness, then that is what we will reap. For that reason, we need to put up our boundaries to protect our spiritual and physical real estate from the misuse of people, places, and things assigned to corrupt our beautiful character and draw us away from the promises of God.

Just know that the measure of love and respect we have for ourselves will determine what we allow in our lives.

In the end, without boundaries, it's safe to say that anything is bound to happen. So it is wise to establish them from the start of every relationship and situation. Now, if you happen to lack a sense of self-worth, I suggest you research the life of Jesus Christ. I am confident that this will open your eyes and heart to the immeasurable value God sees in you.

BOUNDARY TIPS

To learn more about boundaries, you can view the "Getting What Your Worth" e-course under the resources tab at www.marshellebarwise.com. This course provides very practical guidelines to identify unhealthy connections and tips on how to properly establish boundaries to protect and preserve the beautiful value you possess. Believe me, we are worth it.

DECLARE: God thank you for allowing me to see that your boundaries are beautiful and for my protection. As you help me identify any areas of my life where I've failed to put the proper boundaries up, I promise to take action to set those borders to protect the priceless value You have given me.

CAPTURE YOUR BEAUTIFUL THOUGHTS

What are some areas, activities, or people in your life that God is revealing needs boundaries? What immediate actions do you plan to take to start putting those boundaries in place?

_____

_____

_____

_____

_____

_____

_____

"And He has made from one blood every nation of men to dwell on all the face of the earth, and has determined their pre-appointed times and the boundaries of their dwellings, "so that they should seek the Lord, in the hope that they might grope for Him and find Him, though He is not far from each one of us; "for in Him we live and move and have our being... **Acts 17:26-28**

REFLECTIVE NOTES

CHAPTER THIRTEEN:
THE BEAUTY OF RECONCILIATION

THE PATH OF PEACE.

I grew up in a household of strong personalities. In that environment, everyone, except for my mother, communicated without much concern for how the message would make the other person feel. In fact, we'd make jokes about each other's flaws in a comical manner as if it were a challenge to see who was quick enough to make a witty comeback.

Over time, the way I communicated at home became my method of communication outside of my household as well. As a result, I had teachers and friends pulling me aside to talk to me about not being so *direct* to avoid offending others. I wish I could say that I was responsive, but I wasn't. I would get very frustrated because I felt entitled to speak my mind about anything and anyone. I also felt like no one cared when someone hurt my feelings and made jokes about me – so in my opinion, I had the right to be that way.

All because of my stubbornness, I experienced tons of broken friendship that my pride wouldn't allow me to restore. And although I wanted to change, I'd cover up my true feelings with an attitude. I thought I was protecting myself from getting hurt, but actually, my unforgiving heart was only amplifying my feelings of hurt, bitterness, and all the other unpleasant emotions I carried. Eventually, this unhealthy behavior followed me into adulthood and my faith walk with Jesus.

Now isn't that unusual...I loved God, but my relationship with people was horrible. I was guarded, defensive, and critical. If you are wondering how it could be that I lived like this as a Christian, I must remind you that salvation is a daily walk of surrender (Philippians 2:12). This dysfunctional mindset about other people was just one of the many layers hindering me from expressing the beautiful image of the Heavenly

Father. Luckily, as I pursued a closer relationship with God, He began to speak to my heart and shine a light on this issue. It became apparent that this area of my life had to change. Suddenly the Lord started to bring people to mind that I needed to reconcile with. I struggled with following through because for so long I found comfort in shutting these people out.

Oddly, this behavior gave me a false sense of safety and control. But the truth of God's Word regarding reconciliation started piercing my heart and making me uncomfortable with the sin of unforgiveness.

Scriptures on Reconciliation

"For if you forgive other people when they sin against you, your heavenly Father will also forgive you. But if you do not forgive others their sins, your Father will not forgive your sins." **Matthew 6:14-15**

"Therefore if you bring your gift to the altar, and there remember that your brother has something against you, "leave your gift there before the altar, and go your way. First, be reconciled to your

brother, and then come and offer your gift." **Matthew 5:23-24**

"He who says he is in the light and hates his brother is in darkness until now. He who loves his brother abides in the light, and there is no cause for stumbling in him. But he who hates his brother is in darkness and walks in darkness, and does not know where he is going because the darkness has blinded his eyes." **1 John 2:9-11**

"We know that we have passed from death to life because we love the brethren. He who does not love his brother abides in death. Whoever hates his brother is a murderer, and you know that no murderer has eternal life abiding in him." **1 John 3:14-15**

"If someone says, "I love God," and hates his brother, he is a liar; for he who does not love his brother whom he has seen, how can he love God whom he has not seen?" **1 John 4:20**

"Then Peter came to Him and said, "Lord, how often shall my brother sin against me, and I forgive him? Up to seven times? "Jesus said to him, "I do

not say to you, up to seven times, but up to seventy times seven." **Matthew 18:21-22**

As you can see, those scriptures leave no room to question how important forgiveness is to God. Realizing that God called me to walk in love and be prepared to forgive those who offended me challenged my pride and made me question if I wanted to be "all the way" saved.

I thought it was weakness to walk out a lifestyle of forgiveness, but later found it was a key component to strength and victory. Relationships are the most valuable gift in life. Everything we will ever do and the places we will go are only possible because of the relationships God gives us. Matthew 12:25 tell us "*a house divided cannot stand,*" so our unity with God, others and ourselves are vital. Even more, we never know who God has designated to help push us into purpose – and if we choose to hold onto unforgiveness, we could get detoured down a dark path of pride. I've learned this first hand too many times. When I'm not mindful, I still fall into unforgiving behaviors because surrender is a choice.

So to experience our inheritance of freedom we need to abandon offense quickly and pursue His perfect peace habitually. Don't let the offense fester and grow roots. Deal with it while it's on the surface, because once it gets thick, it's that much harder to uproot or navigate through. If you've ever had to pull up weeds, you know what I'm talking about.

As you read this I'm confident that God is going to start bringing people to your mind that you need to reconcile with, don't dismiss these thoughts. God is offering you a roadmap to freedom. If you haven't already, the first two meaningful relationships you should reconcile is the one you have with your self-image and the relationship you have with God. I suggest starting with God because it's typically the easier of the two since the Heavenly Father has already forgiven *all* our past, present, and future offenses – it's just a matter of us receiving His forgiveness. Here is a simple example of how to resolve that:

DECLARE: God today I come to You with a sincere heart and confess that I surrender to Your love and forgiveness through Christ Jesus. I thank You for loving me even when I didn't love you in return. Now I humbly ask that you help me walk in that same love and forgiveness toward others in this life journey.

If you made that declaration from a sincere heart, I believe that you are eternally reconciled with God. Yay!

All right, let's continue on this journey to ultimate freedom. If you've ever spoken negatively about yourself in any way, that may be a good indication that you need to reconcile with your self-image. Sometimes this is a real challenge because we buy into the false truth that people can be perfect apart from God. This simply isn't true. We are all flawed. The good news is that reconciliation with God through Jesus means we are no longer defined by our past. 2 Corinthians 5:17 says, "*Therefore, if anyone is in Christ, he is a new creation; old things have passed away; behold, all things have become new.*" So "New Creation" let go of any offense you hold against yourself for not fitting the perfect mold you were told to be. In Christ, you've been given a fresh start as an image carrier of God in Heaven.

DECLARE: God through Your forgiveness and freedom through Jesus, I also forgive myself of every offense and wrongdoing. Now help me walk in love, patience, and understanding toward my shortcomings knowing that I was crafted by You and for You.

Now I suggest that you sit quietly for a moment and allow forgiveness to sink in. Reflect on the truth that you are NOT your past. You have been forgiven and redeemed from every impure thought and act. The fear of rejection cannot hold you captive anymore because God's love has made you eternally accepted and free from the condemnation of sin. You have been sealed as His kingdom heir forever. Receive that and believe that, because it's yours.

As always, we want to rejoice with you in every victory, so if you took a step of faith to reconcile today – please send us your story. See the back of the book for details.

Okay, let's keep moving down this road of reconciliation. For us to make peace with others,

I've provided a very useful outline on how to reconcile with someone in a healthy manner. I've personally used this to identify when reconciliation was necessary and as a guideline on how to walk through that process with godly conduct. In honesty, this has never been easy for me, but the final results have always been worth it.

Some Signs You Need to Reconcile:

1. When you hear reconciliation or forgiveness, this person comes to mind.

2. You find it hard to pray for that person.

3. You will not refer, recommend, or endorse this person for something they are qualified for - which would be a blessing to their life.

4. You avoid this person when you can, or this person commonly avoids you.

5. You have negative thoughts about this person or have spoken negative words about this person.

6. You sense that this person may have something against you.

7. This person has hurt and offended you, and the matter was never addressed, or it was, but the discussion was more of an act and not genuine on both person's part.

Steps to Walk Through Reconciliation

1. Pray – Always pray before you meet with the person or persons that you need to reconcile with. Ask the Lord to make your heart and intentions right before Him. Also, pray for self-control.

2. Timing – Be mindful of the place and time that you approach this person to make amends. Sometimes the wrong location and time can come off confrontational – and you don't want to make room for the enemy to make your good intentions appear as evil.

3. Be Humble – Do not approach the situation or person as if you have all the answers to solve the issue at hand.

4. Take your blame – DO NOT USE "YOU"

statements. Approaching the matter, pointing the blame on the other person will only cause them to become defensive. Instead, be honest about your contribution to the issue. If you feel you did not do anything to offend or intentionally hurt that person, your fault may have very well been not addressing it once you realized that there was an issue.

5. Speak the Truth in Love – Do not avoid the major issues that resulted in the friction to begin with.

6. Be Silent – Hear the other person out. If the person starts to speak words of offense and attempts to point the blame at you, do not respond offensively – instead just be silent. This will allow them to hear themselves. Once you can speak, remain apologetic for your contribution to the issue and keep solution focused.

7. Speak Life – Leave that person with words of encouragement and peace. Tell them what God says they are "this does not mean being preachy" – such as saying, "the bible says"...just be genuine and uplifting.

8. Forgive – Do not speak about the issue or that person in a negative light anymore. Also, do not discuss your meeting of reconciliation in terms to make yourself seem like the "Bigger person." If at anytime you get the urge to speak negatively about that person, pray for them instead and also pray for your heart to continue to heal beyond that issue.

9. Be Wise – If you honestly believe that meeting in person with someone can result in physical harm, just walk through these steps of forgiveness in prayer and ask God to heal your heart toward them.

Now that you've read through the above, I encourage you to quietly sit and allow the Lord to reveal anyone that you need to reconcile with. As the names come to mind, write them down as a commitment that you will follow through with the call to reconcile. Trust me, once all necessary forgiveness and offenses have been resolved you will experience the greatest sense of peace. And if that alone isn't worth it, according to the word, you will also experience a more effective and powerful prayer life.

Note: Reconciliation does not mean that you have to engage in a close relationship with that person. It is simply a call to lift the burden of offense and replace pain with peace through forgiveness. By no means do I encourage relationships that are abusive in any manner. If that is your situation, be wise, and if necessary, seek sound guidance first.

PERSONAL PURSUIT OF PEACE

"Now all things are of God, who has reconciled us to Himself through Jesus Christ, and has given us the ministry of reconciliation, that is, that God was in Christ reconciling the world to Himself, not imputing their trespasses to them, and has committed to us the word of reconciliation. Now then, we are ambassadors for Christ, as though God were pleading through us: we implore you on Christ's behalf, be reconciled to God." **2 Corinthians 5:18-20**

_____

_____

_____

_____

_____

DECLARE: I receive your call to daily walk in the ministry of reconciliation to freely extend the same forgiveness you have given me to others. Thank you in advance God for giving me the strength to put aside my pride and pursue reconciliation with anyone I've offended or been offended by. Through it all, I ask that you be my shield of protection to guard my heart against any intentional abuse due to my kindness. Today, no matter what, I make a sincere commitment to stand firm in the beauty of reconciliation.

If you took the leap of faith to practice reconciliation, congratulations! I can only imagine how much lighter your heart feels now that it's not harboring offense toward someone. If you've only completed a portion of your list, there is no such thing as partial freedom, so I encourage you to see it all the way through. You can do it!

REFLECTIVE NOTES

THE FACT OF THE MATTER

YOU ARE NOT ALONE.

The world will continue to provide a vast amount of products promising to help us achieve lasting beauty. And yes, those products may help us appear more visually appealing, but none of them have the capability of producing real beauty.

Real beauty is an attribute of the heart, and cannot be undone. It is something that illuminates from the inside out. Beauty is seen in how we treat other people, including ourselves. Beauty is demonstrated in how we talk and through the choices we make every day. Real beauty is eternal, unfading, and found in the presence of God.

If we choose to daily surround our lives with peace, joy, love, and the Word of God, we will see the fulfillment of beauty start to evolve in our lives. We will even start to see it rub off on others.

The best thing about eternal beauty is that no one can take it away from you. Unlike our physical beauty, not even time can undo the beauty that you glean from a sincere connection with God. So I encourage you to daily set your focus on Him as the source of all things good, including your beauty, which was intended to extend the bounds of time.

DECLARE: From this day forward I declare that I am no longer the same. Although the change may not be seen with the physical eyes, my heart has been made new. My desire is to shine from the inside out and make the development of my character a priority. I will seek the treasures of Heaven that do not perish and put my hope in the Lord at all times. I do not have to chase society's standards anymore. Through Him, I have been made free to excel to the greatest and highest measures possible. God in You I find beauty and the ability to make a lasting difference in the world that cannot be undone. Amen!

†

This may be the close of the volume, but it's definitely not the end of the journey. I believe that our best is yet to come! So cheers in advance to all God will do in you and through you. May we both finish this journey with great joy.

Your Friend,
Marshelle

FIRST TIME RECONCILIATION GIFT

If you made the declaration to reconcile with God for the first time, Congratulations! You are now a part of the worldwide Kingdom Family. To celebrate this monumental moment with you, I want to give you a small gift of remembrance.

To claim the gift, please visit our website link www.marshellebarwise.com.

If you have any friends or family members who already believe in Jesus, don't forget to share the good news with them. I'm certain they will be thrilled to celebrate with you!

QUICK REFERENCE

FOUNDED IN BEAUTY

Declaration: My existence was formed in beauty. Beauty is a part of my nature!

Scripture Reference: *"He has made everything beautiful in its time. Also, He has put eternity in their hearts, except that no one can find out the work that God does from beginning to end."* *Ecclesiastes 3:11*

†

CHAPTER ONE: THE TRUE MEASURE OF BEAUTY

Declaration: I am the apple of God's eye and He defines my beauty. So today, I vow to walk this journey by faith and trust in the Lord's ability to complete the beautiful work He Himself started in me.

Scripture Reference: For *the LORD does* not *see* as man sees; for man looks at the outward appearance, but the LORD looks at the heart." **1 Samuel 16:7**

CHAPTER TWO: THE BEAUTY OF TRANSPARENCY

Declaration: I am not ashamed to resemble the glory of God because I am a descendant of His greatness. For He is the source of my eternal beauty.

Scripture Reference: Therefore, putting away lying, *"Let each one of you speak truth with his neighbor,"* for we are members of one another. **Ephesians 4:25**

†

CHAPTER THREE: THE BEAUTY OF YOUR TESTIMONY

Declaration: I have overcome by the blood of the Lamb and by the word of my testimony. No matter the test, I vow never to give up on God and believe that He will never give up on me.

Scripture Reference: *And they overcame him by the blood of the Lamb, and by the word of their testimony; and they loved not their lives unto the death.* **Revelations 12:11**

†

CHAPTER FOUR: THE BEAUTY OF BEING GENUINE

Declaration: I am His workmanship, created in Christ Jesus for good works, which God prepared beforehand that I should walk in them. **Ephesians 2:10**

Scripture Reference: *For His eyes are on the ways of man, and He sees all his steps.* **Job 34:21**

†

CHAPTER FIVE: THE BEAUTY OF DEVOTION

Declaration: I will walk in the beauty of devotion and take authority over my emotions by guarding my senses from the bait of unhealthy *sin- sations*.

Scripture Reference: *If anyone among you thinks he is religious, and does not bridle his tongue but deceives his own heart, this one's religion is useless.* **James 1:26**

†

CHAPTER SIX: THE BEAUTY OF DISCIPLINE

Declaration: I will not allow myself to be deceived by the sin-sations of this world. I will guard my heart, mind, soul, and emotions against perversion and seek out the truth through God's Word.

Scripture Reference: *But I discipline my body and bring it into subjection, lest, when I have preached to others, I myself should become disqualified.* **1 Corinthians 9:27**

CHAPTER SEVEN: THE BEAUTY OF FAITHFULNESS

Declaration: No matter how I feel, I will remain faithfully devoted to the Lord. I will submit my will and watch Him bring me out victorious

Scripture Reference: *If we are faithless, He remains faithful; He cannot deny Himself.* **2 Timothy 2:13**

†

CHAPTER EIGHT: THE BEAUTY OF THE TRUTH

Declaration: Lord, I will no longer live in fear and allow shame to define who I am in this world. I declare that I am your beautiful creation and I will live by your truth to display what you declare about me. Now I ask that you fill me with love for your truth, so I can grow into the likeness of Christ my Redeemer and the Savior of the world.

Scripture Reference: *For the LORD is good; His mercy is everlasting, and His truth endures to all generations.* **Psalms 100:5**

†

CHAPTER NINE: THE BEAUTY OF HUMILITY

Declaration: I set my heart to understand and to humble myself before God, so He will hear my words and send angels to war on my behalf. *(Daniel 10:12)*

Scripture Reference: *But he who is greatest among you shall be your servant. And whoever exalts himself will be humbled, and he who humbles himself will be exalted.* **Matthew 23:11-12**

†

CHAPTER TEN: THE BEAUTY OF COMPLETION IN CHRIST

Declaration: In Christ, I am complete, and I have no reason to compete. There is a plan, purpose, and assignment for my life. I am already blessed because God made me and I believe I have access to unlimited resources from Heaven. So, Lord, thank you in advance for all the answered prayers and fulfilled promises that lay ahead of me. I know that those who wait on You will not be put to shame.

Scripture Reference: *Then the Lord answered me and said: "Write the vision and make it plain on tablets, that he may run who reads it. For the vision is yet for an appointed time; but at the end it will speak, and it will not lie. Though it tarries, wait for it; because it will surely come, it will not tarry.* **Habakkuk 2:2-3**

†

CHAPTER ELEVEN: THE BEAUTY OF ORDER

Declaration: God I put you first and trust that you are aligning my life with your perfect will.

Scripture Reference: *But seek first the kingdom of God and His righteousness, and all these things shall be added to you.* **Matthew 6:33**

†

CHAPTER TWELVE: THE BEAUTY OF BOUNDARIES

Declaration: God thank you for allowing me to see that your boundaries are beautiful and for my protection. As you help me identify any areas of my life where I've failed to put the proper boundaries up, I promise to take action to set those borders to protect the priceless value You have given me.

Scripture Reference: *"And He has made from one blood every nation of men to dwell on all the face of the earth, and has determined their pre-appointed times and the boundaries of their dwellings, "so that they should seek the Lord, in the hope that they might grope for Him and find Him, though He is not far from each one of us; "for in Him we live and move and have our being…* **Acts 17:26-28**

†

CHAPTER THIRTEEN: THE BEAUTY OF RECONCILIATION

Declaration 1: God through Your forgiveness and freedom through Jesus, I also forgive myself of every offense and wrongdoing. Now help me walk in love, patience, and understanding toward my shortcomings knowing that I was crafted by You and for You.

Declaration 2: I receive your call to daily walk in the ministry of reconciliation to freely extend the same forgiveness you have given me to others. Thank you in advance God for giving me the strength to put aside my pride and pursue reconciliation with anyone I've offended or been offended by. Through it all, I ask that you be my shield of protection to guard my heart against any intentional abuse due to my kindness. Today, no matter what, I make a sincere commitment to stand firm in the beauty of reconciliation.

Scripture Reference: "Now all things are of God, who has reconciled us to Himself through Jesus Christ, and has given us the ministry of reconciliation, that is, that God was in Christ reconciling the world to Himself, not imputing their trespasses to them, and has committed to us the word of reconciliation. Now then, we are ambassadors for Christ, as though God were pleading through us: we implore you on Christ's behalf, be reconciled to God."
2 Corinthians 5:18-20

ABOUT THE AUTHOR

Marshelle Barwise resides in Arizona with her husband, Carlos Barwise. Marshelle is a Bible college graduate from Arizona Christian University (formerly *Southwestern College*) , and she has served youth, young adults, and women for the last 12 years in her community and various parts of the country. Through the gift of arts and public speaking, Marshelle desires to encourage and empower others to live the beautiful journey God has wrote for them.

To learn more about any of her upcoming projects or request to have her join your next event, please visit www.marshellebarwise.com. She'd love to connect with you!

If you opted to step out and start your journey to embrace your eternal beauty, please message us at www.marshellebarwise.com under the "Take the Journey" tab. We look forward to hearing from you.

Attention "Aspiring Writers" keep a look out for some fun creative workshops.

SOCIAL MEDIA

FACEBOOK – Marshelle.Barwise

INSTAGRAM – @marbarwise

YOUTUBE – Marshelle Barwise

WEBSITE: www.marshellebarwise.com

• COMING SOON - VOLUME II •

Share your Eternal Makeover story for a chance to be featured in the next volume or our upcoming video series. Your story could inspire someone's life, and we'd love to help you make a difference.

www.ingramcontent.com/pod-product-compliance
Lightning Source LLC
LaVergne TN
LVHW011201080426
835508LV00007B/534